Hum

Hum

JAMAAL MAY

ALICE JAMES BOOKS
Farmington, Maine

11 10 9 8 7 6 5 4 3 2

Alice James Books are published by Alice James Poetry Cooperative, Inc.,
an affiliate of the University of Maine at Farmington.

Alice James Books
114 Prescott Street
Farmington, ME 04938
www.alicejamesbooks.org

Library of Congress Cataloging-in-Publication Data

May, Jamaal.
  [Poems. Selections]
  Hum / Jamaal May.
    pages cm
  ISBN 978-1-938584-02-2 (pbk.)
  I. Title.
  PS3613.A948H86 2013
  811'.6--dc23
                    2013022185

Alice James Books gratefully acknowledges support from individual donors, private
foundations, the University of Maine at Farmington, and the National Endowment for
the Arts.

ART WORKS.
arts.gov

Cover art: "A Vexing Quiet" by Brian Despain: www.despainart.com.

Contents

Acknowledgments

The author gratefully acknowledges and thanks the following publications in which poems previously appeared:

Another and Another: An Anthology from The Grind Daily Writing Series: "If They Hand Your Remains to Your Sister in a Chinese Takeout Box"

Atlanta Review: "Triage"

Blackbird: "Man Matching Description" and "Ask What I've Been"

Callaloo: "Pomegranate Means Grenade"

The Collagist: "If They Hand Your Remains to Your Sister in a Chinese Takeout Box," "Macrophobia: Fear of Waiting," and "Thinking Like a Split Melon"

The Cortland Review: "Mechanophobia: Fear of Machines"

The Drunken Boat: "The God Engine"

Foreign Policy in Focus: "Pomegranate Means Grenade"

The God Engine (Pudding House Press Chapbook Series, 2009): "Chionophobia: Fear of Snow," "Coming Back for You," "The Boy Who Bathes the Dead," and "Paper Crane on Letting Go"

Gulf Coast: "On Metal" and "Thalassophobia: Fear of the Sea"

The Hairpin: "Hum for the Bolt"

Indiana Review: "Athazagoraphobia: Fear of Being Ignored"

The Kenyon Review: "The Sky, Now Black with Birds" and "The Hum of Zug Island"

The MacGuffin: "The Girl Who Builds Rockets from Bricks"

Mead: The Magazine of Literature and Libations: "Aichmophobia:
Fear of Needles"

Michigan Quarterly Review: "A Detroit Hum Ending with Bones"
and "Hum of the Machinist's Lover"

Minnesota Review: "The Man Who Paints Mountains and
Helicopters"

Muzzle Magazine: "I Do Have a Seam" and "Neat"

New England Review: "And Even the Living Are Lost" and
"Hum for the Hammer"

The Normal School: "Hum for the Stone"

The Paris-American: "On Gentleness" and "Hum of the
Machine God"

The Pedestal Magazine: "Paper Frog on Spring"

Ploughshares: "Masticated Light"

Poetry: "Hum for the Bolt"

Sixers Review: "How to Get Your Gun Safely Out of Your Mouth"
and "How to Disappear Completely"

Southern Indiana Review: "Looks Like a Boy" and "Paper
Tiger to Wind"

Spoon River Poetry Review: "Still Life"

Many thanks to the many friends and colleagues who made this collection
possible through creative, logistical, and emotional support including
Reginald Dwayne Betts, Tommye Blount, Veronica Castrillon, Nandi
Comer, Kahn Davison, francine j. harris, Khalid El-Hakim, Quincee

Herbert, Melissa Roberts, Anna Saini, Erin Shaughnessy, Laura Swearingen-Steadwell, Scheherazade Washington, Jasmin White, and Team Turgid: Roger Bonair-Agard, J.W. Basilo, Tom Budday, and Karrie Waarala.

Thank you to the organizations that fed me in multiple ways: The Stadler Center for Poetry, Shara McCallum, Andrew Ciotola, and G.C. Waldrep; Terry Blackhawk and the Inside Out Literary Arts Project; the entire Cave Canem family, Alison Meyers, Toi Derricotte, and Cornelius Eady; Ross White and the Daily Grind Writing Series; Callaloo Writers Workshop, Dr. Charles Henry Rowell and Gregory Pardlo; Poetry Slam Incorporated and the poetry slam community; Lynn Procope and the NYC LouderArts Project; Team Fucking Nuance; Michael Collier and the Bread Loaf Writers Conference; the MFA Program for Writers at Warren Wilson College, Ellen Bryant Voigt, Debra Allbery, and Amy Grimm; Alice James Books, Meg Willing, Carey Salerno, and the cooperative board for believing in this collection and showing that belief at every turn.

Thank you to Vievee Francis and Matthew Olzmann, the two hardest working and most generous poets I know. They may have done more for my writing life than even I have.

Special thanks to the careful eyes that gave these poems no quarter: Alan Shapiro who guided me in laying the foundation that became *Hum*, Gabrielle Calvocoressi for challenging me on form and endings, C. Dale Young for the revision philosophy and thoughts on organic ordering, Rick Barot for the title and his macro to micro insights, Catherine Barnett for her fresh perspective and finishing touches, Carl Phillips for his guidance and big picture advice, and Tarfia Faizullah, the first, last, and closest reader of every kobita.

And thanks especially to the May family for making me the rare poet whose craft is respected and encouraged by all of his kin: my father Claude, mother Sytoria, brothers Jabari and Jared, and my twin sister Danielle, who believed in my poetry before I even began writing it.

*Dedicated to the interior lives of Detroiters
and the memory of David Blair*

Still Life

Boy with roof shingles
duct taped to shins and forearms
threading barbed wire through pant loops.

Boy with a safety pin-clasped
bath towel of a cape
tucking exacto knife into sock.

Boy with rocks. Boy
with a metal grate for a shield.
Boy with a guardian

daemon and flawless skin.
Boy in the shuttered district,
a factory of shattered vials,

green and brown glass.
Boy with a tiny voice
and crooked cursive handwriting,

with bent nails in a pouch,
metal flashing scavenged in bits,
with half a neck tie

tied around the brow
pushing a fire door wide.
Boy with a boy living

in his head kept quiet
by humming a lullaby
of static and burble.

The boy in the boy's head
watches sparse traffic
from a warehouse window

and takes notes on where
overpass paint hides rust,
where the cyan bubbles up

into a patchwork of pock
and crumbling disease,
a thief in the bridge's body

he doesn't see, but knows
is coming tomorrow
to swallow his song.

Hum of the Machine God

There isn't much to discuss with the Machine
God, though its voice is hard to ignore;
it speaks in planks of wood shaped for the sea,
sputters smoke, eats grass. It speaks in snow
spit into piles, commands the motion of a needle
through a hem. It hums. It waits.

Once, in a parking lot, it spoke to the boy waiting
for an exchange between a sewing machine
and his mother to come to a close. Mother's needle-
skilled fingers had already learned to ignore
pain, but the boy's hands were supple. The snow
under Father's idling car became a sea,

running into drains towards another sea
the boy hoped and hopes is out there waiting.
Almost heard it one morning, shoveling snow
as a neighbor's open garage rattled with machinery,
boatbuilding tools, a thrum he knew to ignore.
Father said, *Might as well build that boat with needles,*

but the spell held the boy. To watch the needling
of a board through a notch was to see a wooden sea-
dragon and dream of riding it away. *Boy, don't ignore
me.* A lip split open. *Shovel.* Father hated waiting
and had even less patience for the broken machine
coughing exhaust in the yard, clutching a snow-

colored stone in its throat. Yes, he prayed the snow-
blower would take Father's hand. Yes, the needle
of Father's scream, as a thumb was machined
clean off, brought icicles down. The boy listened for the sea.
Gripped his shovel. Gripped his oar. Now, in a waiting
room, he bows to the florescent hum and begs. *Ignore*

my prayer, goes his stupid little prayer, *please ignore*
my voice. The thumb in a jar packed with snow,
will take a miracle for doctors to reattach. Waiting,
as if to plead, *Let me try my hand, give me the needle,*
Mother taps a knitting needle against the sea-
foam-colored formica, rapid as a machine,

but the Machine God, still busy with the lights, ignores
the needle's morse code prayer while the boy waits
for snowmelt in his mouth to taste of oak and sea.

Athazagoraphobia
Fear of Being Ignored

I used to bury plum pits between houses. Buried
bits of wire there too. Used to bury matches
but nothing ever burned and nothing ever thrived
so I set fire to a mattress, disassembled a stereo,
attacked flies with a water pistol, and drowned ants
in perfume. I pierced my eyebrow, inserted
a stainless steel bar, traded that for a scar in a melee, pressed
tongue to nipple in a well-lit parking lot, swerved
into traffic while unbuttoning my shirt—
                                        There is a woman
waiting for me to marry her or forget her name
forever — whichever loosens the ribbons from her hair.
I fill the bathtub for an enemy, lick the earlobe
of my nemesis. I try to dance like firelight
without setting anyone ablaze. I am leaning over
the railing of a bridge, seeing my face shimmer
on the river below — it's everywhere now —
                                        Look for me
in scattered windshield beneath an overpass,
on the sculpture of a man with metal skin grafts,
in patterns on mud-draggled wood, feathers
circling leaves in rainwater — look. Even the blade
of a knife holds my quickly fading likeness
while I run out of ways to say I am here.

How to Disappear Completely

You are quarter ghost on your mother's side.
Your heart is a flayed peach in a bone box.
Your hair comes away in clumps like cheap fabric wet.
A reflecting pool gathers around your altar
of plywood subflooring and split wooden slats.
You are rag doll prone, contort,
angle and arc. Rot. Here you are
a greening abdomen, slipping skin,
flesh fly, carrion beetles. Here
where bullets found shelter,
where scythes found their function, breath lost
its place on the page, where the page was torn
out of every book before chapter's close.
This is slippage, this is a shroud of neglect
pulled over the body, this
is your chance to escape.
                            Little wraith,
bend light around your skin until it colors you clear,
disappear like silica in a kiln, become
glass and glass beads, become
the staggered whir of an exhaust fan,
a presence only noticed
when gone. Become origami.
Fold yourself smaller
than ever before. Become less. More
in some ways but less

in the way a famine is less.
We will forgive you for not being
satisfied with fitting in our hands.
We will forgive you for dying to be
a bird diminutive enough
to fit in a mouth without being crushed.

Man Matching Description

Because the silk scarf could have cradled
a neck as delicate as that of a cygnet
but was instead used in last night's strangling,
it is possible to marvel at the finish on handcuffs,

because I can marvel at handcuffs
pummeled by stones until shimmering,
the flashlight that sears my eyes
is too perfect to look away, because

a flashlight has more power on a southern roadside
than my name and blood combined
and there is no power in the very human
frequency range of my voice and my name is dead
in my mouth and my name is in a clear font on a license
I can't reach for before being drawn down on,

because the baton is long against my window,
the gun somehow longer against my cheek,
the vehicle cold against my abdomen
as my shirt rises twisted in fingers
and my name is asked again—I want to
screech out, *Swan! I am only a swan.*

The Sky, Now Black with Birds

If I say riot helmets outnumbered the protesters
who, after Troy Davis was executed, stuck around
to throw useless punches into the courthouse grass
while a woman near the forest of batons
lay sprawled facedown in the lawn gripping a Bible,
a green sea beginning to memorize
the shape of her grief—If I say *Death,*
cure death, and had such power over the scythe,
how many cranes would it take to lift her
out of this drowning?
       If I tell you
Lawrence Brewer was executed
five hours earlier for the murder of James Byrd—
if I ask you to look for birds foraging
between Brewer's intricate tattoos,
I don't mean to distract you from the cross
that still burned on his arm that day.
I don't expect you to stare into a graffiti
of iron crosses and spider webs scrawled
across flesh and find a thrush vibrating with birdsong,
but I want you to know why I listen for more
than the cawing of crows:
       I wanted Brewer dead.
So dead, my tongue swelled fat with hexes, so fat
I wonder how *forgive* could ever fit inside my mouth.
Somehow it's always there, fluttering in the larynx
of Ross Byrd—the man whose father was dragged,

urine soaked, by Brewer behind a truck.
Watch him say it.

                    Forgive.

I swear,
the word has feathers. I want
to learn to get its wings between my teeth
before more retribution
blots out the sky.

                    When I tell you
glare flickered off a cop's visor
and startled a single crow away
from the murder that flapped the sky into inky pieces,
I want you to watch close enough
to notice the feathers aren't black at all.
Like bruises and ink, they are
only this full-bodied purple—purple so rich
your eyes will still swear it's black the next time
you see it spread out across sky. Watch it
spread like the flush of pancuronium bromide
into diaphragm, watch close enough to pinpoint
when the muscles lock.

                         If it is said the injection
is humane, we mean to say this
is humanity: no crack of rope, jerk
of limb, no bloated face, clenched jaw, or reek
rising twisted in smoke from a cooked torso—
we mean to say there is nothing to disturb
the nest between our ribs, there is nothing
to make a heartbeat rumble
like a murder of so many wings.

Looks Like a Boy

Here in pants with a permanent crease, a boy fidgets in his uniformed hell surrounded by desks filled with fidgeting students who are surrounded by cinder block walls and black-grated windows—as if they could keep him here. They do keep him here—they've got him surrounded. He's surrounded by mouths, mouths that won't shut up, mouths that want to suck him in, suck him dry. He looks like he needs the girl with chewing gum in her hair, like he won't forget which drawer his cap gun was thrown into. Notice how the walls always look like they're trying to get closer to the walls. He looks like he's not worried about toys anymore, like he's taller this week and smirking more, like he's been in this grade before and he could go another year.

He looks like he could fit this entire class under his tongue. Watch his tongue. How it moves. How it makes a boy back down, makes a grown man think twice before striking him in the face. How it makes the girl weep. How it makes the girl moan. How much this looks like love. This could be love. He loves like an amateur, hugs her tight to get her breasts against his abdomen. He looks like he doesn't need the girl, like he's going to eat the girl up. His mouth is huge now, especially when he's eating. Or laughing. Laugh with the boy with the big beautiful teeth. Laugh at the boy's beautiful mouth, lips so full they are an insult. Insult the boy who looks like he never wanted friends, never wanted anything he couldn't fold and stuff down jean pockets. It looks like he's not going to class today, like he won't be enrolling this fall, like he's got a pistol weighing him down. Looks like a full-grown man from this distance. Down the street from the wreckage left by last night's storm—live wire flicking like a dare, a tree cracked in half by lightning—he's down there, in the drizzle, keeping warm, gun cold under a puffy coat filled with feathers.

A Detroit Hum Ending with Bones

Glass above my bed trembles
at the touch of bass pouring thunder-thick
out of twelve-inch speakers and I almost don't mind
being jolted awake because I know this song.
It's not a favorite song, but I know it. Sometimes
just knowing a pattern is plenty. Sometimes
I need more rattle from the cabinet, more
whir from the fan spinning in the laptop
warming my twin sister's lap—
and when that's not enough,
I might take off my shirt and press
my shoulders against a refrigerator—
one of those beige monsters
from the 80s you can really feel
working for its hum.
                                    A humming bird draws
nectar in my thoughts, wings beating
80-something times per second
but there aren't many flowers here; it's been many
summers since I stopped even listening for bees.
I know my cell phone near a hive
can confuse insect signals,
a natural technology too outmoded
for a message vibrating in my pocket to not
make a drone go haywire
and spiral into the grass.
                                    Is that enough?
Then what about your Chrysler that idles

so hard the tickle scurries from thigh
to earlobe? There's always a hymn
waiting for ears. A Tibetan singing bowl
looking for an audience. A vibraphone
begs to collide over and over
with the yarn-tipped mallets you hold.
And even when you were young and smirking
and the clerk was definitely afraid of you,
the tremble of his hand made your change clink
out the notes of a small tune
made of fear, just for you.
                              Do you remember the key
of the plastic kazoos in choir?
Do you remember elementary science?
We were taught to read an entire sentence
before trying to fill its blanks
and began to say *umm*
as a placeholder for answers, as in:
"Hearing, the only sense that is completely mechanical,
occurs when sound travels the _*umm*_, vibrates
your eardrum, and is amplified by the _*umm*_,
which is a group of tiny bones."

On Metal

Hmmmmm, drags at the back of a throat
and becomes *mmmhmm,* when three men huddle
around a car, admitting some smaller defeat,
while not quite admitting the emergence of digital

parts means this won't be solved by ratchet alone.
No one is happy to learn what an afternoon of chafed
knuckles, metal on skin, no longer solves. What can't

be pulled from the steel tangle under a hood.
It's as though they found the wrench that could set
free a bike from its training wheels only to discover
their daughter has had a driver's license for years.

I clap the man at the center of this trio on his shoulder,
not quite hard enough to shake loose a cigarette
dangling almost acrobatically from his lips and say,

I'll just take it to a dealership and be done. I say it as if this
is not a huddle—like I'm not a team manager plucking
the ball from my pitcher's glove early in a game
that falls near the wane of an otherwise solid career.

Detroit's building 'em like robots now, he concedes, slams
the hood and rattles the chassis. He's probably right,
considering the clank of metal closing on metal,

but I still can't help thinking of how much the frame
is like my frame. The mystery of my Chrysler's right side
not responding—silent speaker, head lamp dead, window
sealed shut, frozen power door lock—is no more

mystifying than my left ear's limited frequency range
or the left eye I'm now told is blind by a doctor
who huddles over me to assess some unknown damage.

Damage that is ongoing. A diminishment I'll live with.
I don't get cars, but I get this: how difficult it is to get
a wreck off cinder blocks and why my dad once fiddled
daily with a dead Camaro, refusing to believe its silence.

Masticated Light

In a waiting room at the Kresge Eye Center
my fingers trace the outline of folded money
and I know the two hundred fifty dollars there
is made up of two hundred forty-five I can't afford to spend
but will spend on a calm voice that can explain
how I can be repaired. Instead, the words *legally blind*
and *nothing can be done* mean I'll spend
the rest of the week closing an eye to the world,
watching how easily this becomes that.
The lampposts lining the walk home
are the thinnest spears I've ever seen, a row of trash cans
becomes discarded war drums, and teeth
in the mouth of an oncoming truck
want to tear through me. Some of me
always wants to be swallowed.

∿

The last thing my doctor said before I lost
my insurance was to see a vision specialist
about the way light struggles and bends
through my deformed cornea.
Before the exam I never closed my right eye
and watched the world become a melting watercolor
with the left. Before a doctor shot light
into the twitching thing, before I realized
how little light I could handle, I never
thought much of the boy who clawed up at me

from beneath my punches, how a fingernail scraped
the eye, or how it closed shut
like a door to a room I could never leave.

⌢⌣

I could see the reflective mesh of his shoes,
the liquor bottle tossed in an arc
even before it shattered at my feet, and I am embarrassed
at how sharp my eyes were, how deft my body,
my limbs closing the distance—how easily
I owned his face, its fear and fought back tears—
all of it mine. I don't want to remember the eyes
that glanced over shoulder just before
I dragged him like a gazelle into the grass
that was a stretch of gravel and glass
outside a liquor store. How easily this becomes that.

⌢⌣

On a suspension bridge I close my bad eye
and it's like aiming through a gunsight;
even the good eye is only as good as whatever glass
an optometrist can shape. I watch sundown
become a mouth. Broad and black-throated,
it devours the skyline and every reflection.
Horns sprout from the head of my silhouette
rippling *dark, dark, dark* against the haze of water
and I try to squint that monster
into the shape of a man.

On Gentleness

Tell me I once came close. That your body wasn't
an obelisk and mine, so much wire wound
around wire. I will always wonder

if I can take you, know you will always be stronger,
and marvel at how you appear even larger
than before with my niece cupped

in your tattooed arms. I know something simple
provokes you to call: a comic book
we've both read, a good time

to visit, but my thumb hovers over *decline*
and I hold my breath before I press
against the waiting *answer*.

Before I left for Florida—a week after I tore
the collar of my shirt twisting out
of your grip, a week after

I disappeared with our shared car, the Venture
minivan we nicknamed Vendetta,
and brought it back to you

empty and smashed—you stopped to tell me
never come back. You meant it. I said
I wouldn't. I meant flinching

is something I'd only do in oncoming light, never
in the overcoat of a shadow; being the size of
a threat did strange things to my tongue.

Tell me about the night I hurled a phone receiver
at your head and the orb of blood on your lip
seemed like it'd never fall, how you

bound me by a wrist, bruised my ribs against the floor,
and never threw a single punch. Wasn't that
a kind of gentleness, Jabari?

Chionophobia
Fear of Snow

Fluttering ash dissolves on your brother's tongue.
He thinks of you building a fort from snow

before you knew what forts were
and he could stand in your footprints

without touching the sides.
Can two snowflakes be the same

on a ghost-white street where enough gather
to construct faceless snowmen? In this desert,

sand blinds the way snow did back home.
Your brother patches holes

in men with names he can't or won't learn,
and wonders if, somehow, you are still here,

using an earthmover to pour sand
into foxholes. Do you still hear soldiers claw

at the shifting weight of their fresh graves,
or are there only silent arms and legs

in your dreams, bent like strange flowers?
Is the sun a flash grenade? This heat

is so heavy the fruit stands buckle and ripple
like mirages, but your brother shivers

remembering your mother's shiver,
the way she sank to the ground, heavy

with news, and your body comes home again.
Your bone-colored casket repeats

its descent, sinks under the flag, and a thud
resounds. Fades. He still hears it.

The rub of your snow pants, the fallout
of snowball fights, every ice-ball slapping

garage, snowflakes dragged in circles
by wind, until they blur like a sandstorm—

he hears it all. Deafening like footfalls
against the icy driveway, resonant

like your mother's voice, calling
the wrong name—your name—again.

The Boy Who Bathes the Dead

The boy decides soldiers can no longer be dead,
       so he begins to dig.

Graves are shallow enough that, using only his hands,
       he quickly finds a limb,

buried without a corpse. He brushes dirt away,
       slides the arm into the pocket of overalls.

Until all soldiers are found and placed
       in separate ziplock bags,

his fingers rake soil,
       churn the dark earth. His brother

finds him afterwards filling a sink to rinse
       the crevices and metal joints, worried

he bathes the plastic infantry too carefully.
       As if they had families. As if they were men.

Thalassophobia
Fear of the Sea

for David Blair

Tonight, you are sweat-itchy and drunk.
    Your guitar sleeps under black felt

in a case under Cinco de Mayo's black sky.
    Your laugh pours like thick honey. Your arms

open, the gap between your teeth opens
    and I am uncomfortable as only you

can make me. You stubbled kiss.
    You friction against cheek. You taught me

how to kiss my father and I am less forgetful
    as you made me, though forgetful enough

not to exhale when sleep wraps
    coral around my throat until my lover

wakes me, choked with nothing
    and I tell her I am drowning.

I fill toilets and sinks and rugs
with bottles of whiskey I can't quite hold
in the empty thing that is my belly. I pour
and swallow and pour and swallow
and pour it all back into my cupped hands.

Tomorrow, I will still be reckless
just like you taught me, and though I still itch

at the thought of wet clothes clinging to skin,
I long to hug you after a performance
before the night air evaporates the proof
of that work from your back. I want to believe
water is just water—what you said that day
the sky turned dark-aluminum above us. You said it
as though nothing had ever been warped by rain.

In this last dream, there is no rigging
          to get tangled in, no water to rush

down our throats. My hand
          is uneasy on your leg, my head against

your shoulder. You don't find it heavy
          at all. You're singing.

Everyday the shells you left behind remain
clean, though no one is left to rinse
the sediment away. Who should have such a job?

Somewhere between your wake and a new town
I can't call home, I slept in a bathtub

with the clock radio cranked loud enough to be heard
over the thundershower because I couldn't sleep
in my car for another night, and the bed

in that motel room was lumpy and dream-soaked,
and you know how I am: Blair,

I want everything to happen at dawn,
            sand between toes and plum light

on the water. You know
            I get like this sometimes—I listen

for footsteps that will never come,
            remember waves I've never seen,

watch them fold and break and slowly
            whet stones that jut up from coastlines,

and today I learn something old
            about the sea. Even the conch is a bit

of a blade, coiling itself around itself,
            spiraling to a point, so that all we find

lovely in its folds forms
            the outline of a dagger.

Coming Back for You

Tonight the tide will stretch out. Syringes
and splinters of glass will be collected.

Shells and stones that aren't needed
until morning will be left cleaving beach.

You'll forget that sound in a month
then remember it on a runway waiting

for your ears to pop. In Pittsburgh
a vat overflows and scalds a foundryman

while a young chef somewhere smothers
a fire because she lost control of it.

In a backyard, a boy learns a boomerang
doesn't come back to you, only your location;

if you should be elsewhere when I return
I may be lost, twirling out of view, while

exhaust hurries from a bus in Michigan
hurrying a bouquet of passengers from an airport

to the missed. An arm scratched red.
A zippered pouch full of cures. An addict

who can't stop picking at his face
rolls a scab between fingers

for the remainder of the trip. You watch him
while stroking a cowry on the necklace I strung

in Oregon. A pair of teenagers too frightened
to head home fall asleep watching dawn,

the Pacific comes ashore to reclaim a hermit crab
finding only the shell, immovable where it rests.

Hum of the Machinist's Lover

There is zinc under your
breastplate, copper in your
throat. I polish your steel

to a shimmer before
even considering
the music. Your tutu,

a nickel-plated half
circle with pleats hammered
one by one. Eyes flicker

like flashlights are behind
them because flashlights are
behind them, wired to

panels, triggered by my
touch. Place your cold pincer
against my fleshy palm,

lean forward on your wheels.
In a voice like cotton,
hum us a melody

from the speaker box I
soldered to your belly.
It's fine if you're afraid.

Tell me where it aches. Tell
me where rust encroaches—
I know what oxygen

does to your surface—How
could I not? I am breath
and air and air.

Hum for the Hammer

Be held. You will be unable
to hold back, and it will be
necessary to get used
to the downward swing,

anticipate the strike and love it,
if for no other reason than to love
the upward swing and sturdy
rhythm that accompanies the ting.

Be hickory or ash, straight-grained
and strong enough to survive overstrikes—
one miss could snap your neck.
May sandpaper be the rough

hand that rubs you smooth.
Be carved until the end of you is a wedge—
you already know the precision it takes
to fit well enough not to be dislodged.

Be a length of carbon-rich steel,
2,350° F in the open flame
before you are positioned between
two dies, let the pressure have

all of you until you are formed.
Have the flash cut from you;
excess is excessive. Be cooled in water,
not air. Don't breathe. Drown.

Neat

Hidden by the overhang of a circular bar,
lies a man who's seen the bottom of his tumbler.
No one is above being invisible,
not even me, with my shirt tidily pressed,

another man who's seen the bottom of a tumbler.
Each swirl of scotch nudges closer to the rim.
Not even my shirt will stay tidy and pressed,
my tie cinched and secure. It's waiting to unravel.

Each swig of scotch nudges me closer to a rim
every day, drops roll off the cliff of my parted lips.
My tie cinched and secure, I'm waiting to unravel,
waiting to spill into sleep—joints sore and speaking.

Day drops off a cliff. My lips part,
I drool on scuffs and bruises from boot and heel.
What I spill seeps, joins the floor, speaking
about straight shots taken to the head.

I'm all scuffle and bruises barely healed.
A swallow of whiskey won't drown my questions.
Another shot won't take me out of my head.
Why do I dress with this much care?

Swallow whiskey? Drown in questions?
Why a beard so prepared, ensemble so neat?
Why dress this carefully?
Why bother to drag a razor through the shadow

of a beard, prepare, assemble, neatly
tie a loop with no beginning or end, only
to be a bother, a draggled, razor-thin shadow,
hidden by the overhang of a circular bar.

How to Get Your Gun Safely Out of Your Mouth

Go ahead and squeeze, but not before you put on some tea, clean two cups, lift shades and pin back curtains. Not before the end of this song, before dawn reaches in, before you turn the page or a woman apologizes for dialing the wrong man again—not before you learn her name, how to pronounce it, how to sing it with and without regret catching in your throat—Are you done? Go ahead and squeeze after the hinges are reinforced on all doors, the house secure from storm or intruder, your laces tied, this commercial break over, drywall taped, spackled, painted—a nail driven, a painting hung and adjusted—there is still so much to adjust, arrange, there is still time—and you write your letter, correct every letter, scrawl the signature so swift and crooked it becomes the name of another—relax the jaw that holds the barrel in place, remove gun, point to heaven, and squeeze until the clip is empty like the chamber.

And Even the Living
Are Lost

Pigeons scrap over a crust of bread while feathers
fall into filthy runoff water. The gutter spits them
down the throat of a sewer. The sewer gives us nothing,
the curb at least returns the dice.

Today, it is meaningless to look for your fist,
there, shaking until the rattle of bones
sounds like winning. You wanted to see clean water
someday, eat sambussa in Ethiopia and fumble
a foreign tongue. Now, in prison, you are as far away
from Dexter Ave as you've ever been.

Yesterday your son pressed his nose to the screen door
to watch a gaggle of baseball caps crowd the sidewalk.
The bones did what bones do.
Streetlights buzzed with their particular sadness.

The last night of your last free summer, streetlights
added a sickly orange glow to the shimmer
of guns, slippery with sweat, so your son could see

the casual havoc of it all. He watched the teeth
of handcuffs close around your wrists the way
a perched bird watches: quiet, flinching at slight sounds.

∿

The dice game erupts, a bottle shatters, a door slams shut
and the sound ricochets off pavement, darts off
like some worried pigeon while your son stares at us.
How long has he been staring at us?

Aichmophobia
Fear of Needles

Understand, uncle, I learned the plunger
of a hypodermic needle fit neatly in the hands
of action figures before the first time
I had my blood drawn.
Maybe this is why I couldn't make sense
of my sister's trembling legs as we waited
for the crooks of our elbows to be needle-kissed.
There's so much I didn't know then:
how much fear I needed to carry,
the definition of *skin flute*,
why the back of my hand was struck
after I found, lying in woodchips,
what I thought would make a sturdy sword.

Because I didn't know the welts on your arm
pulsed to show where a belt dug in,
I only compared them to my mother's
red markings—a shoulder punished
by a tote bag loaded with books.
Now I know the groceries I helped deliver
across the threshold of a stale motel room,
the bread and sandwich meat in my hands,
were part of the contract that ensured
you'd never be able to explain to me
what bends and burns you like a spoon,
crushes you against the floor, what apparition
haunts you, whispering up your arm,

"Become my petite opening,
        itching wound,
my collection of used-up veins.

My wraith, I've studied
        your chasms.
None are too great. The answer

to the question
        your rolled up sleeve asks
of God is yes. He does

have a point. I have come
        to stitch all
this torn sky back together."

I Do Have a Seam

and you see it, there for you

    in the center of my chest, or strings

to pull, a chrome zipper,

    interlocking throat to sternum,

a hollow from belly to thigh,

    or there is only a hole, barely

large enough for your

    opening. Come soon,

puncture. Pull apart until

    my halves billow open, and

muscle, sinew, and organ are

    right there, pulsing

awake in your room. Woman,   here

    within reach, woman

with plump thumbs,

    with slender fingers—

woman I'd fail for—

    hello, you

careful seamstress, you

    needle in my sternum—

stitch my selvage as it frays,

    you know how ragged I've been,

but do you know how

    and why I've always wanted

to be thread, spooled through

    the sewing machine of your hands.

Triage

A suture would be useless
and a tourniquet can't choke off
blood when it spills
from this far up the inner thigh,
so the medic tells PFC _____
his hand will stay there,
pressing on that strip of fabric.
He promises the scarlet flag,
once surrender-white, will manage
to hold him firmly to the world.
He tells him sandboxes are filling up
with the trucks and bulldozers
of the soldier's children
and army men with green heads jutting
from the sand. He repeats *I won't let go*
whenever mortar fire whistles near
the field tent and the limbless
come on gurneys
from the fires. The flowers
are snapdragons; there is a garden
he will raise. As singed paper
flutters around them
like a veil-black snowfall, he has to
remind the soldier about the earth's ability
to give life, to recover
from tilling and burning, about rivers

that fill seas that fill oceans
that throb with the electric blue
seahorse and ambling crabs.
The medic tells him, over the scrape
of men dragged off, some still twitching
with life, that he too will live—
another lie woven into the gauze
he's been winding all day.

The Man Who Paints Mountains and Helicopters

for Rodney Denne

You are not the choice,
no matter what it looks like today
even if the canvas calls you *survivor*
or *whole*. Remember there was no omen,
no rocket-shaped cloud to say
two Black Hawks would fill up
with the living only to be emptied
of the dead by your platoon
who went on foot
because you asked for a coin toss,
because you called it in the air
and nothing you can call god
or fate held that coin in its fist,
turned that face towards sky.

You say nothing divine
guided your hands into the debris
as you sorted metal from man
and found only wreckage,
rifled through fused dog tags
and welds of limbs, wondering
who began where. How
were the rifles connected? I know

you see yourself in one of the two
doomed choppers, somewhere
in those few seconds between
first explosion and second.
You would've known the friendly
beacon was switched off, the Hellfire
missile was locked on,
and that there was a rumble of machinery
next to you a moment ago.

I know a coin spins in your mind
as you paint a moon beyond
the summit. As you tuck two boys in,
their smiles like fault lines,
as you turn down sheets
that will twist into twine around
your limbs by morning, remember
you are not the tail or head
of the coin. Rodney, you are
the spinning, you are the coin's ridge,
you are what happens between
sand/soil/clay and sky.

Hum for the Stone

Here on the shoulder
of a freeway, rebar exposed
by a semi that crushed a concrete
dividing wall to avoid crushing
a hatchback protrudes from slabs
in a way she imagines bone can.

The girl is doing this again:
pressing a malachite
into his palm, her cupped

hand closing his around
its smooth, worthless form.
She whispers kiss-close,

The Book of the Dead says
we'll be falcons with wings
made of this stone.

A boy feels a broken brick
strike between shoulders.
The next stone breaks
against his nose as he turns,
and if not for the many ribbons

of blood sliding between
fingers, one could think
he was doubled over
with laughter, celebration
in the convulsions.

The black tourmaline she polished
is pushed into his pocket.
This one comes in many colors

that make it easy to confuse
with other stones. That's why
it doesn't have a legend—

He removes it to finger
the surface. Crude, glossy,
looks like it could spill.

—except for black. Black
is always easy: all crow and funeral.
Will you carry this to mine?

Clang and clang is the stones' ricochet
off corrugated steel and shields
made from garbage can lids.
The bricks in their hands fit
into a row of pavers on a path
to a garden that grows gravestone.
Some come here to bless barrow-dirt
or to listen for the sound pebbles
make: a lack, a hole opening
at the center of this crumbling din.

The Girl Who Builds Rockets from Bricks

finds no voice louder

than hers in the caverns
       of deserted houses

or overgrown lots that surround
       her excavation for spare parts:

shards of a whiskey bottle, matches,
       anthills erupting from concrete

seams, the discarded husk
       of a beetle. The shells of vacants

reflect the echoes of her little
       song—a song with lyrics

assembled in a quiet language
       only she speaks—language

not spoken with tongue but hands
       that snatch up fists of grass,

crunch into dust the driest leaves—
       small hands that fill jelly jars

with broken glass, gravel, and fire ants,
        each jar, an engine for a rocket.

Rainwater spills from a gas can
        down between bricks, the girl

begins her countdown
        without thinking of a destination.

Mechanophobia
Fear of Machines

There is no work left for a husk.
Automated welders like us,
your line replacements, can't expect
sympathy after our once bright
arms of cable rust over. So come

collect us for scrap, grind us up
in the mouth of one of us.
Let your hand pry at the access
panel with the edge of a knife
silencing the motor and thrum.

Come rummage through our guts
among fistfuls of wire, clutch,
pull until the LEDs go dark.
Our insides may be the jagged
gears of clocks you don't realize

function until your blade gets stuck.
The current that sparks, scrambles up
fingertips, hurrying to your heart
will not come as a hot, ragged
light—you won't notice when it arrives.

There is always a way to touch
the core inside and disrupt
the flow of electric pulses.
Whether the plexus leaks or bleeds,
it can be bled of its vim.

You fear the chassis that was struck
by lightning can't be wholly crushed.
You should. Fear radios left in scrap
yards still twitching with the circuit
and hum of our mechanical hymn.

Pomegranate Means Grenade

The heart trembles like a herd of horses. —Jontae McCrory, age 11

Hold a pomegranate in your palm.
Imagine ways to split it. Think of the breaking
skin as shrapnel. Remember granada
means pomegranate and granada
means grenade because grenade
takes its name from the fruit;
identify war by what it takes away
from fecund orchards. Jontae,
these are the arms they will fear from you.
There will always be at least one like you:
a child who gets the picked-over box
with mostly black crayons. One who wonders
what beautiful has to do with beauty as he darkens
a sun in the corner of every page,
constructs a house from ashen lines,
sketches stick figures lying face down—
I know how often red is the only color
left to reach for. I fear for you.
My heart trembles like a herd of horses.
You are writing a stampede into my chest.
This is the same thumping anxiety that shudders
me when I push past marines in high school
hallways, moments after their video footage
of young men dropping from helicopters
in night vision goggles. I want you to see
in the dark without covering your face,
carry verse as countermeasure to recruitment videos,

and remember the cranes buried inside poems
that hung in Tiananmen Square—
remember because Huang Xiang was exiled
for these, exiled for this, the calligraphy of revolt.
You stand nameless in front of a tank against
those who would rather see you pull a pin
from a grenade than pull a pen
from your backpack. Jontae,
they are afraid.

The God Engine

When I find a dead frog in the freezer,
I have to question the wisdom
of telling my niece GE stands for God Engine:
a mystical device, a suspended animator
that keeps strawberries plump and peaches
fuzzy as fly-dotted pears rot,
corpse-soft on the table.

I imagine the amphibian drifting
on a lily pad down the Puddle Styx.
Maybe I covet youth's fantasies
that spring up like wolfberries.
Why else would I lie?
Maybe I'm the cruel uncle,
forcing her to prepare a shoebox casket
and line the sides with wads of tissue
crumpled damp with tears.

When the burial plot is smoothed over,
I drag a trowel across my jeans
until it shines enough to reflect
the lines multiplying on my face
and consider telling her the truth:
all will reach the pear's destination,
decay is a constant ferryman, and if forgotten,
everything in this freezer will burn.

Paper Frog on Spring

Green begins to stain trees again,
      dark-eyed juncos invade branches.

The sun sears sky, while children
      with their horrible grins fill playgrounds

where dugouts face off like foxholes
      and the fences do nothing.

Bats are dragged through gravel.
      Brims of helmets shade eyes.

Imagine if it happened every year,
      if every April, from any window, friends

dissolved, ran down into storm drains,
      or were absorbed by the greedy lawns.

What if annually you relived the waning
      of a life in spring?

The resurrection rituals:
      barbecues, birthday parties,

saplings that shatter soil,
      emerging from some grave full of us.

Thinking Like a Split Melon

In a sixth grader's notebook
      only two lines are written:

        I go outside. I look at the stars.
           Then I'm sad because of death and stuff—

At a funeral when I was her age, I punched
      dots into the program with a bow
           compass then held it to the light

to trace paths I drew between holes.
      Those constellations. The paths
           drawn between neurons. Their firing

      is how I think.

She adds in pencil

      the castle of the mind is full
           of hundreds of bright specters—

and I wonder what's going on in her head
      and mine. *What sky did we fall from?*

sounds like an appropriate question,
      when I think about it

but it's too much to ask a child, right?

～

Outside, I ask a steel sculpture
          ascending from the depths
                    of museum grass if I am
                              contextualized by its immensity.

The bending blades of grass
          told me it's not appropriate
                    to ascribe words—

which become ideas,
          and soon become my ideas—

to them, as they've done nothing wrong.

          The wind says
nothing
          we can't figure out on our own,

I said, but no one was talking to me.

～

A melon falls from a bag,
          a platoon of ants pours in
                    and out of its gash,

and I wonder if it takes being broken
          open and emptied
                    to be filled with something new.

Didn't a poet say cracks are how light gets in everything?

I'm probably mixing that up.

But this is how I think. Give me a box,
  and I'll fill it with dirt
    or fill it with water
      or fill it with both

and trouble that mire

    with whatever stick I happen to find.

If They Hand Your Remains to Your Sister in a Chinese Takeout Box

If an urn won't do because ceramics
are not biodegradable and you need your ashes
buried in the plot next to your estranged wife
where you can help her feed the worms,
nurture soil, and lift trees into the sky—

If your obit is scrawled on notebook paper,
ripped out and photocopied,
rigid edges and all, and lines still show up
faint like soap scum collected
on a mirror above the motel sink
you were found slumped beneath—

If they hand your remains to your sister
in a Chinese takeout box, give thanks
for the giggling of your niece and give thanks
for this moment when, after tearing
a liquor-stenched wound down the middle
of this family, it for once won't be mentioned

as they gather. Take solace that the plastic bag
carrying you to the cemetery will,
instead of joining you underground,
spend decades holding hands with a breeze
wandering around some landfill somewhere
repeating in bold red font,

THANK YOU
THANK YOU
THANK YOU
THANK YOU
THANK YOU

Paper Crane on Letting Go

Your friendship with wind
     may be the difference

between playing with fire
     and teaching it to dance

like chiffon
     your hair blown wild.

You learn to recognize the sound

but can't describe the rustle
     of your deciduous head.

Pull the past behind you
                like a silk kite

     and the secrets of flight and nest
will escape you

     even as fall sheds along the lawn
and you calculate

the leaves' volume
     from a window.

Measure the value of seeds
        carried earth to earth

in your pockets
            their weight and shape

        the lives of lives
you bury everywhere

and viceroys will whisper
        the myth of you

to cocoons
        and the smallest of us.

I haven't counted
            the universes

that collapse when you sneeze
        verses that flitter

when you open your mouth
        but your lightning-strike laughter splits

the sky when you do
        and I know your generosity

will be rewarded by the breeze
        that tugs at your kite

the breeze that knows

        you will relent.

Hum for the Bolt

It could of course be silk. Fifty yards or so
of the next closest thing to water-to-the-touch,
or it could just as easily be a shaft of wood

crumpling a man struck between spaulder and helm.
But now, with the rain making a noisy erasure
of this town, it is the flash that arrives

and leaves at nearly the same moment. It's what I want
to be in this moment, in this doorway,
because much as I'd love to be the silk shimmer

against the curve of anyone's arm,
as brutal and impeccable as it'd be to soar
from a crossbow with a whistle and feel

a man switch off upon my arrival, it is nothing
compared to that moment when I eat the dark,
draw shadows in quick strokes across wall

and start a tongue counting
down to thunder. That counting that says,
I am this far. I am this close.

Paper Tiger to Wind

Come attack me then

        here

in the stone garden

        when no one

is watching.

        No one

ever watches. My eyes

        never

meet yours

        and when they try

it is like turning to face a shadow

        and as you've heard

of shadows

        they turn

as we turn. Our dance darkens

        into a cyclone

moving counter to clock

        in sync

    with Earth's rotation.

As fluid.

    As ceaseless.

        That is when you will strike.

Won't it be you

        old friend

who finally comes

            to tear through my lungs

     and fling me out over the fields?

I've seen you crouched in trees

      heard you
          settle in the aching

branches of a cherry blossom
      before scattering

             its petals.

My angry-sweet wind
        the waiting you stir

is a scent I have come to crave.

Macrophobia
Fear of Waiting

I love too many women is not the best lead-in
for a conversation that will end
with me telling you I love you
for the first time. And this might not be
the best first date topic. I know this,
but I know it the same way
twelve-year-old me knew the firecracker
in my hand would be a dull burst
lost in the grass if I let it go too soon—
I'm asking if you are like me.
Do you let go too soon? Are you afraid
more of having hands covered in ash
than you are of getting the timing wrong?
This is stupid, but I couldn't wait

to tell you everything
about the stranger, who after pushing
a peppermint over my teeth with her tongue,
told me she never wanted to leave
the listening range of my rambling.
This meant a lot coming from a wanderer
who would never have to hear it again;
I was booked on a plane that had already boarded
when a voice calling my name over the PA
reminded me I could not afford to wait for a later flight,

and ever since, I've been wondering
what runway my hesitation will invoke next,

wondering if it was bad timing
to finally ask for the dance I promised
after you had already become a twirling body
and nervous hand spilling rum across
someone else's shoes? I get it, you got sick
of your life standing like a loaded gun—
everyday with me another hangfire. This wait
isn't foreign to any of us. This wait is a friend
splitting blinds, looking for his cliché of a father.
It is a foot pressed against the door
of a locked closet. A girl stands in line in the rain
holding two concert tickets and this
is what rattles us, the space after
a question mark. Blood work and CAT scans.
What man faces a firing squad
without eventually longing for an exit wound.
This is stupid, but I was afraid to tell you

I kept fiddling with my phone through dinner
because I was fascinated
that every time I tried to type *love*,
I missed the *o* and hit *i* instead.
I live you is a mistake I make so often,
I wonder if it's not
what I've been really meaning to say.

I want to say there is patience at the center
of every firework I hear bloom
from my balcony, signaling the end
of a Tigers game, but I can't see them.
The second floor isn't high enough. Clouds
above the taller buildings flicker, reflecting
their light, so tonight I'm going to watch that instead.

Make an evening of it. A dinner date
with myself and a bowl of handmade guacamole
from Honey Bee Market, and this time
I'm going to wait
to find out if one, just one,
can get high enough for me to see it explode.

The Hum of Zug Island

In Windsor they blame it on machines
across the Detroit River. Residents can't ignore
the low frequency hum taking the shape of a sea-
serpent on oscilloscopes. Beyond gray snow,
plastic bags, and crushed hypodermic needles,
Zug Island is humming—waiting

the way the organs in me are waiting.
My body is a building full of machines,
some more complex than others: needle-
nosed pliers, pistols, a satellite—all ignoring
my commands to sit still. The snow
wants to kiss us, I hear my skin say. The sea

pouring from gutters toward the sea
that must be out there waiting,
eardrums covet the rushing. *Just snow-
melt*, I say to the thrumming machines,
but my voice is easy to ignore.
So I find myself drawn again to needles

of light through drawn blinds, needles
of wind through a window's failing. A sea
of all the outside I try to ignore,
the hum that won't calm and won't wait.
This oscillating piston of a heart, the machine
that should know better, wants to see snow

tremble. It goes on about this rumor of snow
vibrating on that island where old factories needle
into the sky. You can hear it, a machine
that doesn't know it's dead sending a sea
of pulses across shore because it's tired of waiting
for someone to talk to, tired of being ignored.

I know they want to answer it. *Don't ignore*
what I tell you about circuit boards and snow,
I say to my jittery metal friends. I know waiting
is a hand closing slowly around needle
points, but we need the patience of a frozen sea.
Sometimes those words quiet the machines,

the hum gets easier to ignore. But pine needles
still fall gold. Dead trees creak. A rain-gutter sea waits,
machine-gray, and my throat begs to drink the snow.

Ask What I've Been

I think cast stiff
around ankle, plaster poured

into a chest-shaped mold.
I think wet cement.

I say stone, and you think pebble
in stream or marble

fountain or kimberlite.
I say gravel or grave

or ask me later. There are days
I mourn being built

from this. Made
of so much aggregate

and gravestone, so little
diamond and fountain water.

When I was a construction
crane, my balled fists

toppled buildings of boys,
I rifled through the pockets

of their ruins.
Ask what I've been. Detroit

is a stretch of highway littered
with windshield,

a boy picking the remains
of a window from his hair.

I say Detroit;
you think glass.

I say glass; you think atrium;
I say atrium beams

warped by heat;
think cathedral. My shoe soles

say stain. Glass between treads,
treads imprinted on gum.

Everything finds its bottom,
say the sewers.

Don't come any closer,
begs a map of collapsed veins,

while the burnt-out colonial,
this empty lot,

this alley-dark cavity
all say the shelter is sparse, yes,

but there is space here for bones—
a ribcage, brimming like yours.

Recent Titles from Alice James Books

Viral, Suzanne Parker
We Come Elemental, Tamiko Beyer
Obscenely Yours, Angelo Nikolopoulos
Mezzanines, Matthew Olzmann
Lit from Inside: 40 Years of Poetry from Alice James Books,
    Edited by Anne Marie Macari and Carey Salerno
Black Crow Dress, Roxane Beth Johnson
Dark Elderberry Branch: Poems of Marina Tsvetaeva,
    A Reading by Ilya Kaminsky and Jean Valentine
Tantivy, Donald Revell
Murder Ballad, Jane Springer
Sudden Dog, Matthew Pennock
Western Practice, Stephen Motika
me and Nina, Monica A. Hand
Hagar Before the Occupation | Hagar After the Occupation,
    Amal al-Jubouri
Pier, Janine Oshiro
Heart First into the Forest, Stacy Gnall
This Strange Land, Shara McCallum
lie down too, Lesle Lewis
Panic, Laura McCullough
Milk Dress, Nicole Cooley
Parable of Hide and Seek, Chad Sweeney
Shahid Reads His Own Palm, Reginald Dwayne Betts
How to Catch a Falling Knife, Daniel Johnson
Phantom Noise, Brian Turner
Father Dirt, Mihaela Moscaliuc
Pageant, Joanna Fuhrman
The Bitter Withy, Donald Revell
Winter Tenor, Kevin Goodan

Alice James Books has been publishing poetry since 1973 and remains one of the few presses in the country that is run collectively. The cooperative selects manuscripts for publication primarily through regional and national annual competitions. Authors who win a Kinereth Gensler Award become active members of the cooperative board and participate in the editorial decisions of the press. The press, which historically has placed an emphasis on publishing women poets, was named for Alice James, sister of William and Henry, whose fine journal and gift for writing went unrecognized during her lifetime.

Designed by Pamela A. Consolazio
LITTLE FROG DESIGNS

Printed by Thomson-Shore
on 30% postconsumer recycled paper
processed chlorine-free